The Fight Within

The Fight Within

✦

A Story of Women in Recovery

Norma Miller

iUniverse, Inc.

New York Lincoln Shanghai

The Fight Within
A Story of Women in Recovery

Copyright © 2005 by Genesee Council on Alcoholism and Substance Abuse, Inc.

iUniverse books may be ordered through booksellers or by contacting:

iUniverse
2021 Pine Lake Road, Suite 100
Lincoln, NE 68512
www.iuniverse.com
1-800-Authors (1-800-288-4677)

ISBN-13: 978-0-595-35817-5 (pbk)
ISBN-13: 978-0-595-80282-1 (ebk)
ISBN-10: 0-595-35817-9 (pbk)
ISBN-10: 0-595-80282-6 (ebk)

Printed in the United States of America

Contents

ABOUT THE COVER

The front cover is a photograph of the quilt which is the product of an art therapy project led by then art therapy intern, Amanda Salmeri, MS. In this project, each woman was asked to design a quilt square using symbols that represent how they define themselves as women and each square tells a very personal story. For example, one woman used a rose, its leaves and its buds to define herself and her relationship with her children. Still another woman states that a star represents her freedom and her family while for still another the square is about reaching inside to visually communicate her inner feelings. For all, it was finding out they really could create something of which they were proud.

The quilt has been matted and framed and is on display at Genesee Council on Alcoholism and Substance Abuse in Batavia, New York.

A NOTE FROM THE EXECUTIVE DIRECTOR

This book has been a collaborative project with contributions from the women who have shared their life experience telling their stories and sharing their art-work. They are the most important contributors to this project. They share often-heroic experiences of their battles with addiction. In the telling of their stories they share their struggles and victories in such a way that they add under-standing, strength, and wisdom to their lives and to those who learn from them.

In addition we would like to recognize the work of many dedicated GCASA staff. They include Marybeth Reger for secretarial support, Jeff Copeland for design and editing, and Amanda Salmeri, art therapist, for encouragement and therapeutic skills. In addition, our gratitude goes to Shawna Murphy, M.A. and Linda Rost for their guidance with the creative process and to Norma Miller, MA, CASAC, who worked with the women to make it possible for them to tell their stories in this format. Without Norma's vision, writing, organization, coor-dination, perseverance, hard work, and determination, this book would never have been given birth.

Carl Jung said that every addict is a creative genius gone awry. When people get into recovery, it is such a blessing to see their creative genius get channeled into constructive and productive directions.

We hope that you will be as blessed in the reading as we have been in the writing and development of the book you hold in your hands.

David Markham, LCSW

The Fight Within

Life's been so long a journey
Mostly filled with pain
Loss is such a normal part
That nothing else seems sane
Looking for the good in life
And wondering where it's been
Fighting for the things I have
Since I can't remember when
Will I ever find my way
To my inner strength
See what others see in me
The light within my reach...

"A client gives us a poem that puts words to her pain and takes our breath away."
(6)

INTRODUCTION

The Fight Within—A Story of Women in Recovery grew out of the desire of a group of women to give others in treatment an understanding of the value of the connection that develops within the context of group treatment. They used the framework of *Jayne's* treatment experiences to portray this connection and highlight their own stories.

They write:

What follows is Jayne's story. Jayne is all of us and she is none of us and her story is really the story of our collective journey through treatment. While on this journey, we have shared our often-similar experiences with each other and have come to realize a profound understanding *of* and intimate connection *with* each other's lifetimes. It is our hope that this story will support your journey as well.

"My lifetime listens to yours"

—MURTEL RUKEYSER

Our experiences educate us to help show each other the way. Other's experiences, likewise, will help still others. We need to share our histories…there is no greater honor we can give one another than rapt attention. We each want to be heard, to be special, to be acknowledged. and recognition may well be the balm that will heal someone's hurt today.

—Jonathan Diamond

OUTPATIENT TREATMENT

My name is Jayne. I am an alcoholic and an addict. I am all of you and I am none of you.

I grew up in a family where we drank beer like lemonade and no one used the words alcoholic or addict. But my mother drank every day and kept company with a much used and soon to be empty bottle of painkillers to help her through the "tough times".

I guess I don't know my mother very well but then I am not sure she knows me very well either. Dad—oh he was gone by the time I was three. My mom made up for him in quantity of men. I had several "uncles" who visited throughout the years, some of them on a regular basis.

I am the oldest of three kids. My brother is two years younger and my half sister is five years younger (one of the "uncles" is her father).

Mom worked as a waitress but used her tips at the bar after work to relax. Our uncles helped us financially with what you might call uncle assistance so we lived on public assistance and uncle assistance. Because she was often not home or when she was, was always at least a little bit high, I ended up being a mother to her and to her kids.

I grew up fast in many ways—ahead of my time you might say.

Laura's Story...

They say "children learn what they live" and that is the truth. I need to remember. No matter how committed I was to parenting differently than my mom, I repeated her behavior. Not only as a parent, but as a woman.

As a child I quickly mastered caretaking, people pleasing, and surviving abuse of all sorts!

I learned that when mom was sad she drank beer and felt happy again. When she was happy she'd celebrate by drinking beer and other alcoholic beverages.

I lived through many brutal beatings as a child. This was how I was punished.

I learned that alcohol could take away loneliness for a short time. I learned that I wouldn't hurt inside if I didn't feel.

Being taught to disown my eyes and ears, it was difficult to face the world. My senses became dulled as a child. My voice was stolen; yet today I'm learning to speak.

As a child most of what I survived I was never to speak of. These were the rules and I was not to break them. This became my way of staying safe and gaining approval. I trusted no one—especially my own feelings. See, I learned that what I saw, heard and felt wasn't real. Maybe if I took care of the kids, (meals, laundry, baths, etc.) all would be okay. Maybe Ma wouldn't drink and my home could be calm, good, normal...

Today I have a voice, I feel, I am just beginning to touch life. I hear truths spoken in my special rooms, I am free to feel. I'm working on trust—especially trusting myself. Sometimes when I see and hear things that don't feel safe I can choose to walk away, trusting my feelings.

I am choosing people to experience life and learning to let go of the untrue friend I had in drugs.

Even though I became paralyzed as a child learning how to die, I'm fortunate today. My God is teaching me through others to live. It all begins with love, hope and faith in my God and myself. Today I am learning to heal. Hope is our greatest source of healing.

Laura, Age 34

I grew up fast in many ways—ahead of my time you might say.

Alcoholic mothers talk to you a lot when they are under the influence. I often heard much more than I needed to know. It was a bad place for a child to be.

I first entered treatment at age 28—I had successfully avoided it until then. I went because probation made me. They said I had a substance abuse problem. I said I had a probation problem. I thought my probation officer was out to get me. I was on probation for DWI and possession of paraphernalia.

I remember the night I got my second DWI, I had celebrated my 27th birthday and we went out for a few. Of course *I* drove and when the police officer stopped me for crossing the double solid line, he breathalyzed me—it registered .20. The judge said I had to go for a drug and alcohol assessment. I went to GCASA, and they recommended group treatment. The judge mandated this, and I was assigned a probation officer who monitored my behavior.

I went to treatment, but I was pretty angry. I told them I needed individual counseling not group sessions because I did not like groups. I told them I was a special case. They placed me in a group—-so much for special.

In my first group, I let them all know right up front how tough I was. I told them I was different than they were—I did not have an addiction problem. I had a probation problem—probation sent me here. I remember the group was amused—they did not know me. I was in control of my use. It was easy for me to stop—I had done it many times. The group members weren't buying that because they had been there too.

I later learned in this group that I did not control my addiction; it controlled me.

Some other group members were on probation too or in a drug court. Some had been to jail and others to state prison. Others were frightened of the possibility of jail and/or probation.

Ruth's Story…

I've done it all; house arrest, community service, and rehab. I've been under the law since 1995 for my first DWI. I've been convicted of three DWIs in my life. This sent me to jail and then prison where I was terrified for my life and my family's life. It scared me straight—not to drink and drive when I saw Bedford Hills. Things that I saw and learned in prison I only thought were on TV. But they're real. It tore my heart out to be away from my life.

My life was on hold. I was in prison and I couldn't do anything to help out my family with things that were going on outside in the real world. I missed a lot of things in prison—my daughter's sixteenth birthday and her graduation from school. My hands were tied. Family members died and I couldn't be there; friends died. This place was hell to me. I can't wait to max out so I can be free from the law and can do what where and when I want. Free to not have to answer to someone for what I'm doing, to have my heart back and not ripped out of me. FREE TO BE whole again.

Made me realize that it can happen to anyone. Made me stand up for me and be glad to have family and friends that need and love me for me. I'll have prison life in my head forever and don't want to go back to hell, 'cause outside is heaven to me. I'll never be the same. Thank God that I have my husband who loves me and stood by me through it all. I take day by day and don't want that prison life again. I will not ever go back to prison. I'll have my freedom from parole in a few years.

Ruth, Age 40

At first I stayed away from everyone else. I was quiet and withdrawn and it took time for me to learn to trust. I was tight lipped and in control! I did not know how to ask for help. Who needed help? They asked what made me happy?

Using that's what made me happy—what was wrong with these people? It was all that made me happy. In reality, it no longer made me happy at all.

As I continued through treatment I realized the other group members were my teachers and my peers—we could identify with each other and we needed each other. When I listened to my peers' stories, I heard my own story evoking taunting memories—some to be remembered and some best forgotten.

My first group had seven men and two women. I liked those odds!

I had my first treatment romance with one of these seven men. You better believe he was the most unhealthy of them all but I thought he was wonderful. Mind you, it wasn't that I did not see his faults—it was that I believed I could change him, that he would be different once he realized how much he was loved.

By the time I finished this relationship I had relapsed and we were both pretty outrageous.

It took me only three months to drop out of treatment and as a result to violate probation. The judge gave me a choice—inpatient or jail. So there I was off again to another treatment facility—only this time it was inpatient treatment, a more structured, hospital setting, for 28 days.

INPATIENT TREATMENT

I was afraid. I had reason—my boyfriend had said inpatient was like jail. He should know, he had been to both a number of times. But it wasn't. For me, it was a good experience, or at least as good as anything could be that made me stop using. I learned about my drugs of choice and the effect on my body. I remember thinking "Oh my god, I could have killed myself". At first the attention that the counselors gave us put me off. Eventually, it did make me feel special when they paid attention to me. It helped me through the 28 days.

I met some really interesting people. One woman learned she was HIV+ and left against advice. Two weeks later my group heard that she was found dead from a heroin overdose, from a lifestyle choice.

This really affected the group members and they affected each other. Mary told us of the time she thought she was going to die.

Mary's Story…

I had gone down from upstairs into the living room where my grandmother was. While she was talking to me asking me if I was doing "those drugs", I started getting lightheaded. Then all of a sudden I could see no more. I fell to the couch and laid there not seeing, heart beating fast, panicking. I started praying asking God not to let me die. I promised him I would not do any more drugs. Then I calmed down a little and started slowly coming back. During this time I heard my grandmother screaming saying "What the hell is wrong with you? You're doing those drugs aren't you? I told you to stop that shit."

By this time I started to see again and my grandmother was standing over me. I got up, went back upstairs, walking back and forth in the hallway thinking about what happened, wondering what had happened downstairs, if I was going to die and if my prayer to God and the promise I made was the reason I came back. I was still alive.

Of course at this time I had started to lie to myself, saying no I wasn't going to die. I was just tired from lack of sleep. So it's O.K. that I continue doing that stuff. I wasn't lying to God. Well, what do ya know, I had talked myself right back into doing what I was doing and had made myself feel better about it. Later on down the line I'd told myself that I was going to die if I continued to do these things.

It's now many years later and I finally have gone straight. Still wondering if I was really going to die that night, and why am I still alive. Why did God give me more chances over and over again?

Mary, Age 28

Lani's Story...

Now I lay me down to trip.
I pray the Lord my head don't flip.
If I die while in the night,
God you know I'll try and fight.
I drank, snorted, smoked, pushed and popped,
after awhile I couldn't stop.
I got hooked when I was ten
and now I am high on heroin.
I wake up crying more and more,
to where I cannot see the door.
I stumbled and fell on my bed.
My grandmother and brother thought I was dead.
I'm looking at a man in white.
He said I'll die sometime tonight.
I hear my grandmother weak and crying.
Oh dear God my girl is dying.
Dear big brother, I said,
I am going to die,
when I do please don't cry
I'd tried to tell you,
but it's too late.
Those drugs decided my awful fate.
Tell my grandmother I love her and my baby too,
and look after both of them for me.
I feel it now,
it's time to go.
Before I die let my baby know.
Don't let her do those drugs I did,

it's too damn easy to get hooked on them.
The lights are turning from dark to gloom.
there I am in a hospital room.
A blanket of white covers my head.
Oh dear God they pronounce me dead.

Lani, Age 37

Two of the women in treatment were pregnant. Alicia told us her story. She had been in rehab three times. This time she was pregnant and had been using crack cocaine early in her pregnancy.

Alicia's Story…

One of my most horrible experiences during my use of crack cocaine was last summer. I had just found out I was pregnant and I was already using crack. This particular time my car ran out of gas in downtown Rochester and it was a cold night in September. I was cold, I had no money and no one to call. We went to the bus station to get warm and use the bathroom and I realized I was bleeding. I was about ten weeks pregnant and the most horrible part of this story was that I did not seek medical care and the next day I continued to use drugs and not eat.

I am twenty-two weeks pregnant today and I am so grateful for the program and my sobriety. I can't help but wonder what would have happened if I had continued my use. The embarrassment and feelings of being a really bad person because of my use during my pregnancy seem to haunt me. I can't help but repeatedly ask myself how could I have been so selfish to use drugs while I was pregnant? I try to forgive myself but it just is something that is unforgivable. I have found comfort in knowing that I am powerless over the drug and that if I wasn't an addict I would not have done those things.

Alicia, Age 33

This reminded me of my mother's use again—my brother had fetal alcohol syndrome because she drank when she was pregnant with him.

I liked the group experience but found that I was getting wrapped up in the high drama of the stories. I began to see my story and my recovery as less than—less exciting than…less important than…and finally, less serious than…others. My counselor told me that I might soon begin to see my recovery as less exciting, less important and less serious than others. It was then that I learned how easy it was to go back into denial—to minimize my experience as less than it was soon to be followed by a tendency to justify and blame others again. I knew this was true because I had been thinking "I bet I could have a beer or two and not go back where I was before" or "my problems are different than her's—not as serious."

The group was helpful in this too. One member really stood out—her name was Patty. Patty had been to seven inpatient treatment centers. She told me that it was easy to get distracted by the people here and their stories. She suggested that I begin to focus more on myself and less on others. Patty was a good role model. When she talked, she talked about her experience, strength and hope. She stayed focused on this. She seemed to mean what she said and said what she meant.

I appreciated all of this. I was learning. Maybe there was something to learn after all. I noticed I was beginning to listen differently. I started to ask myself what was going on with me. This helped. I listened with a new ear—to identify with others and to question what it all meant to my recovery.

When I caught myself in denial again, like when I minimized and justified, I stopped. I did not beat myself up. I just stopped.

I began to search inside and find ways to share my story with others. This sharing really helped. It was a big benefit to my inpatient experience. Patty said "listening was learning and sharing was healing". I had come a long way from the woman who started treatment several months ago. It was especially clear now why I had struggled with my probation experience initially and throughout treatment.

Finally I realized that my legal problem was like my condition overall—it had progressed over time and gotten out of control. Inpatient offered me the chance to meet others with more advanced legal histories, such as intensive probation, county jail, state prison and parole.

I met a woman on parole. When I stated that I could not identify with the things she talked about because none of these things had happened to me, she replied "not yet". She assured me if I kept continuing as I was, it could and probably would happen to me. She told me of her journey.

Joyce's Story...

As the steel door slams shut again, the feeling of despair and helplessness comes back again. How could this have happened to me? How could I have ended up in prison and lost everything near and dear to me? What could have made me stoop so low? So insane that I lost everything? Alcohol! I am from a long line of alcoholics! My grandparents on my mother's side had a still! What chance did I have? What chance does my daughter have?

Alcohol, what a Prince of Darkness! What an illusion! I've lost my entire adult life due to alcohol! I could have been something or someone. I could have been successful and have been a professional! I could, I could, I could! Alcohol made me feel invincible! I felt I could do or achieve anything. What a lie! All it did was take me down to the rock bottom of my life.

I sit in this cell and wait to be told when to eat, when to sleep, when to go to class, when to go to my job. The feeling of helplessness comes over me once again and I try to seek the answer in God. I once had a somewhat normal life with my daughter. I once had freedom and a life before. I once thought I was in control of my life. But alcohol was in control! I remember freedom beyond the barbwire fence. I remember laughter, sunsets. I remember love. I remember all the things I took for granted. I remember the sweet smell of honeysuckle and the sound of a bullfrog croaking...

Joyce, Age 37

I really heard her when she said "not yet". I realized I had to start putting some things between my drug use and me or the door would slam shut on my future too.

All of this could be overwhelming. Some found help and hope at AA and NA meetings where they stressed things like meeting attendance, a higher power, a sponsor, choosing a home group, slogans and other tools.

Francine said...

When I go to a 12 step meeting I can hear people share their stories, experience, strength and hope. This gives me courage to go on with my sobriety—makes me feel good that there are people to help me with my problems. I can say I really enjoy life on life's terms by sharing with others that are like me. Without their asking me for anything and just by showing me that we can do this together. I have come to accept my life for what it is. I don't blame anyone for what I did to myself. The program helped me to realize it was my doing and no one else. Blaming others does not change anything. Today whatever I go through or feel I know it is me. It is my problem to solve. I have learned to accept my higher power to help guide me through whatever I need to go though and to help me realize I do not have to be high to go through what life deals me. (See Appendix B—The Twelve Steps)

Francine, Age 43

Another group member, Carolyn, summarized her 12-step experience for the group. She said that it is a program of 12 steps. It does not matter in what order you use these steps. You can work on any step in any order to get your recovery established. In time, all steps are taken. Most folks who are successful work all of the steps in order.

Carolyn had worked the first six steps with a sponsor and was starting on the seventh. She said these steps are a framework for living life and are worked (used) over and over, not just the first time.

Carolyn's Story…

Alcoholics Anonymous and Narcotics Anonymous are 12 step programs with the same basic principal: one addict or alcoholic helping another to stay clean. It's not a club and the only requirement to attend their meetings is the desire to stop using. I think that's part of what attracted me to the program. When I first walked into a meeting I heard a bunch of clichés. The one that really sticks with me is: "Meeting makers make it." To me that means that I need to attend a meeting regularly if not daily for the sake of hearing something that might make a difference in my life.

After going to several meetings and listening to the stories of many people, I chose a person with more clean time and similar experiences to be my sponsor. She and I began to work on the 12 steps together.

The first step was to admit that we are powerless, both over our disease and the drug or the drink. I had to realize that my "sick" behaviors were a part of that disease. I guess "sick" behaviors would include not sleeping for days and taking a drink or a drug to the bathroom with me, because I didn't want to miss anything.

Step two talked about finding a power greater than ourselves to restore us to sanity. This step is difficult for any newcomer. It seems that we all or at least most of us come into the program questioning God. Then, it's brought to my attention that a power greater than myself is not and does not have to be "God."

The third step is to make a decision to turn our will and our lives over to the care of God as we understand him. I guess that means to let what will be will be. I have no control over what other people choose to do. I only have control over my choices and I need guidance, because without it, I've made many poor choices in my life.

In step four we make "a searching and fearless moral inventory" of ourselves. This step is difficult, because it suggests that we acknowledge all of our faults and weaknesses for what they truly are. We start to realize and learn who and what we really are. This list shows us what characteristics we may want to change about ourselves.

Admitting to God, to ourselves and to another human being the exact nature of our wrongs is the suggestion of the fifth step. In doing so we lose isolation, learn humility, gain honesty and trust, and we learn about ourselves.

In the sixth step we find ourselves entirely ready to ask God to remove these defects of character. Only then do we find spiritual growth in dealing with personalities and behaviors. It turns out to be a lifetime job.

The seventh step tells us to humbly ask God to remove our shortcomings.

Carolyn, Age 34

Her guidance encouraged me. As a result, I began to pay closer attention in meetings.

The inpatient staff also urged us to change people, places and things as a vital part of recovery. This meant developing a support network of sober people doing sober things in sober places. The 12-step meetings helped me meet sober people who were working a plan (or program). I really listened to their stories and amazingly heard my story in theirs. I was relieved there were others like me—I did not feel so alone. I had always felt frightened and alone but in the 12 step programs of AA and NA, I felt accepted and connected.

The Fight Within

Life's been so long a journey
Mostly filled with pain
Loss is such a normal part
That nothing else seems sane

Looking for the good in life
And wondering where it's been
Fighting for the things I have
Since I can't remember when

Will I ever find my way
To my inner strength
See what others see in me
The light within my reach

Will I find the peace within
Ever feel that I'm worthwhile
Let go of never ending fear
Invite others to my isle

I've spent hours thinking
Of life's ups and downs
Hiding from it's mysteries
Like faces of a clown

Not knowing what lays out there
Too scared to really look
Keeping safe within my shell
Placed in the corner nook

Having times I'd like to shed
All the fear inside
Yet never being able to
Feeling more than paralyzed

Seeking those who'll understand
Hoping to find just one
Someone I can share with
And when I'm through won't run

Wishing time would ease the pain
Yet realizing that it's there
Trying to release it all
And wish I knew where

Always scared to show the world
All feelings held within
Wondering where I'll end up
Not knowing where I begin

Trying to make things simple
Yet knowing deep beneath
Evil lives inside me
Like bombs with boats to seek

Fear so overwhelming
Not able to let it go
More comfortable with that feeling
Than any others that I know

Ginny, Age 22

I completed my 28 day inpatient stay and left with a good foundation for recovery.

OUTPATIENT AGAIN

When I left inpatient, I went back to GCASA. This time, though, I had a different attitude.

I went directly to Phase II Women's group where I practiced acceptance and learned to receive feedback from others—to listen about my addiction and addicted life style and its effects with an open mind and willingness to change. Phase II is about accepting that this is my problem to live with, to learn what and how to change. I focused on myself in this group as did the other women. With the help of each other, we began to sort out our issues and what was and was not working in our favor about ourselves and our choices.

Many of the women were victims of assault, domestic violence, incest, and/or rape and other sexual assault. One woman was raped when she went to cop heroin. Another woman had stolen from a dealer's stash—he beat her up pretty badly. She said dealers do not like to be cheated and say things like "don't be playing with my money." They tend to hurt anyone who does.

Georgia's Story…

It was summer and I was getting high all day, people were in and out, my boyfriend seemed to have an endless supply. I didn't even ask where and how he got it. Then it was getting to be dark and the people were still coming but I was told to stop answering the door. Once again I didn't ask why, I was too busy getting high. I wasn't even feeling the high because I was smoking for two or three days straight. I was so tired I would just use what I was given and try to be high. So, I'm trying to calm myself and say I'm done. I lay down and try to rest, I hear this banging on my door—real loud banging. The boyfriend says in a scared voice—"Don't you dare answer that door!" Now I finally ask why they're not going away and he tells me that he stole their package and that's what we've been smoking! So now I'm nervous and the pounding is getting louder. We are upstairs and I say "I have to answer; they're not leaving." He tells me to say he's not here.

I'm on my way down the stairs and BOOM my door comes flying open…two men, the first is in with a gun and the second I guess was a door man to make sure no one

15

got out. I grab the guy saying "Stop don't do this!" "This isn't the city", anything I can do to keep him downstairs. He says to me "I'm not looking for you. Where is he?" My boyfriend kicks out the upstairs window, barefoot and goes out into a neighbor's house. She calls police. While the police are coming the two men calmly walk to their car, get in and leave right past the police on their way. The police never caught them, and I don't think they cared to because they know I was doing wrong. I will never forget what danger I put myself into by grabbing the man with the gun. I could be dead today. Thank God I'm not!

Georgia, Age 31

Not all dealers are dangerous males though. Sometimes dealers are female addicts.

Sarah's Story…

Several years ago I started drinking lots of alcohol to be accepted into the "cool" crowd. Then I started smoking weed. At first, my partying was just on the weekends. Then smoking pot became a daily part of my life. It wasn't long before I stopped drinking and became "just a pothead." I was smoking marijuana all day long, including during work on my breaks. A couple years ago, I was introduced to powder cocaine. Sometime in between, I messed around with LSD, psychedelic mushrooms, opium, and ecstasy. When I came across the cocaine, I felt a brand new feeling—stimulants. At first, I was snorting it. Then I was smoking it on top of weed. The taste was incredible.

Early last year, I tried my first rock of crack cocaine, by itself in a glass pipe. I fell in love. It gave me the sensation of the best orgasm that I could ever have. Shortly after that first hit, I stopped smoking pot and snorting cocaine. I was smoking crack throughout everyday, staying awake for up to nine days at a time.

I'm epileptic. Cocaine is a seizure-inducing drug. My use ended very abruptly and took away everything that I loved.

The man I met and married introduced me to the lifestyle I grew to love. I had already been drinking and getting high on the weekends, but he convinced me that I could function normally just being high. That's when it became daily. Then I learned that he was selling weed to his friends and I met his dealer. I began selling to my friends, too. Pretty soon every drug I touched became business. I loved the money. I loved the popularity that I felt. Everyone came to me or my man for all of their needs.

I would take offense to the term drug dealer. After all, I was only working with "friends."

My son got to know all of these friends and my supplier, too. He would be playing video games with them or us or by himself, while transactions and use were taking place in the same room. I warned my son not to tell or to give any inclination that he knew of any drugs, because he would be taken away from us and given to some other family.

Just before this past Christmas, I experienced a cocaine-induced seizure. I was home alone with my son and he was in the room to witness it. In his words, I started to vibrate and I fell to the floor. As I fell, my head hit the table. My lit cigarette landed in my hair and the pill I was holding (actually a crack rock) rolled across the floor. I started to breathe like I got electrocuted; I can only guess that he meant I was hyper-ventilating. Then I just stopped. He said that he tried to wake me up. He tapped on my leg and on my shoulder, "but you just wouldn't wake up, Mom. You passed out right in front of me and you wouldn't wake up. I thought you were dead," he told me during a visit.

My eight-year-old son was the first love that I lost. He ran outside to a neighbor's house and called 911. When I came to, there were social workers and ambulance personnel standing over me. The police were already searching my home and seizing my belongings. I was released from jail on Christmas Eve. It was difficult to accept gifts for my son, who wasn't there. I continued to use and sell the drugs despite losing my child. When it came time to face the judge, I decided to seek treatment. I entered into a twenty-eight day rehab center. That ended my drug dealing business; no more easy income for me. Then I went into a halfway house. My husband was still using. So my marriage ended, too.

It's been over seven months since my first day in rehab. I miss being my child's only caregiver. I miss my husband and the easy money, too.

I now realize that I can no longer live that lifestyle. I am ready to become a responsible and productive member of society. I'm going to be my son's mother once again. My drug-based marriage is on its way to a divorce, and I'm going to attend college to acquire the education needed to operate a legal business. I simply don't want to die a lonely, actively using, drug addict.

Sarah, Age 27

Karen, another female dealer, told us the story of how she was raped.

I'm a young woman who was given a second chance at freedom, motherhood, and life. I was facing drug charges for selling crack cocaine.

I had one of the worst pasts; a father who died when I was five and a mother who did every drug out there. She didn't even know how to be a mom, she didn't know how to love. I truly couldn't stand my mom. What did I do to have a mother that hurt me so bad over and over? I had no answers that made sense to the thousands of questions that ran through my head. My mind was so cluttered with doubts and confusion and that made my heart heavy with guilt and shame. So I sold drugs and did drugs, thinking it was gonna make my problems better.

I always had money, but with that came "haters." I was robbed three times, the last time I was robbed I was at the club and it was by three guys that I thought were my friends. They drugged me up by slipping something in my drink without me knowing. They robbed and raped me that night. It's a night I can't remember, but I'll never forget. The drug made me black out. I had bruises, hickeys, burn marks all over my body and I bled from my butt for ten days. I was on an emotional roller coaster that changed its course without warning or consideration for my mental state. It never asked my permission.

Attacks of depression, despair, confusion, and frustration hit me and consumed me from the bottom of my feet to the tip of my head and every corner and crevice of my body in between. I didn't know how to deal with this, so I got high every chance I had and I didn't care about making money anymore. I was becoming just like my mother. I almost gave up on myself.

The morning after the rape, I felt like I should have died. But God gave me a second chance at life. One month later I went to jail for drug charges and God gave me a second chance on my freedom. Eighteen months later my son is home with me again. God gave me a second chance at motherhood.

I have a lot of clean time to think about what I need to change about my life and me, so I won't feel stuck. I take my second chances as a blessing!

Karen, Age 29

In this group, we also discussed other acts of violence against women, both as children and as adults, such as domestic violence and sexual abuse.

Betty's Story...

I see a little girl very alone, so alone she grew up and found her comfort in a bottle. So many things happened to this little girl, bad things, while she was left alone. Her mother lived in a bar. To this little girl seeing her mom was like visiting someone in jail. To see her she had to go to the bar. This little girl became accustomed to this style of life. When mom did come home she would bring a different man each time, and when she left for work she left this little girl alone with a stranger who molested her. Therefore, this little girl not only found comfort in a bottle, she also found she could block out the pain with that bottle.

How very sad for this girl, how very sad this little girl was. She grew up, but she is still a little girl. A little girl waiting for her mom to come home.

Mom's gone now but she still waits. She no longer wants to feel the pain and she doesn't want to drown out the pain with that bottle. All she wants is her mother's love and to hear the words "I'm sorry". She can't talk to mom now 'cause she's gone, so the pain lives on inside. So this little girl still feels alone, is alone.

Betty, Age 21

Lorna's Story…

I wonder if abuse takes place
In gently running streams
Or does life just move along
As uncomplicated as it seems

Do offspring ever scream or cry
Because of their own adults
Left to feel shame deep within
Layered over with coats

Are their young abandoned
Before taught to survive
Neglected and left broken
When just barely alive

It's hard for me to comprehend
Their simpler way of life
And how a more "intelligent" species
Cause their children so much strife

Lorna, Age 25

Another woman, Joanne, told us she had an alcoholic mom who beat her up emotionally and she cried alone. After one of these beatings, she swore she would never use alcohol or drugs. But she did and this set her up for her chosen lifestyle.

Joanne's Story…

Twelve years old. Who's that kid? He' cute. Tommie, Oh yeah! He's so nice; nice clothes, nice jacket, cute smile. He wants to go out with me. Okay. Mom likes him. He plans on having his own business. He likes to work. He'll take care of me? Yeah, he's nice. Still twelve years old, wait who's his friend? John. Nice leather, so he drinks. Big deal he smokes weed. What, he did acid? Probably a one-time deal. No I've never seen him do coke. I don't believe rumors. He's beautiful. That's why I had sex with him. I know I was drunk, so I told him it wasn't a good idea. He knows more; he's experienced. Tommie will never know.

Seventeen years old. Still with Tommie. I love him. He kept his word. We just graduated—he bought me a car. He works over forty hours a week. We have a cute little apartment and I'm starting night classes. He takes good care of me. Sometimes I get bored when he's working so much. Then he likes to hang out with the guys a couple times a week. Well, I always have John. We've been together on the side since seventh grade. Five years later, we're still together. He must really love me. Tommie loves me too. He just put a huge engagement ring on lay-a-way for me. But John really loves me. He tries to spend very minute with me. But it's hard for him. He's got a couple other girlfriends and he's been drinking and staying up late. I hear he's into cocaine pretty heavy now. He usually finds two to three times a week for us to have sex. Not like Tommie. He doesn't want me as much because he doesn't want sex like John does.

Eighteen years old. Oh, John and I decided we loved each other too much to hide it. I left my apartment, left the ring, the pictures, animals, and the real love of my heart to move in with John and his parents. He loves me. The sex is great. He doesn't hit me like I saw him hit Janice. But she's a nag. Well today I got my first black eye. His parents kept me in the bedroom with ice on my face. Now I know it is so nobody found out. He'll sober up they said.

Twenty-two years old. Pregnant—now he'll stop. He loves me and I'm having his son. We bought all new tables, the other ones got broken. He fixed the holes in the walls. We finally have our own place. Eight months pregnant. It's hard to get him off me. Please stop, you're gonna hurt the baby. Stop.

Little Johnnie is two years old. He's getting bigger. Daddy said he won't hit me anymore. He's getting too old, he'll understand. Then why are we running out the back door barefoot in the snow to the neighbors? They called the cops. Domestic violence. It's just a bad fight. Leave us alone. You don't know us.

Twenty-nine years old. I just woke up. I'm in the hospital. Morphine pump. Last thing I remember is passing out at home, then being loaded into a helicopter from one hospital to another. I was almost dead. He whispered that when he kicked me my spleen ruptured. I'm O.K. now. Don't tell the doctor, I'll go to jail, prison. I won't do it again I promise. I love you.

Joanne, Age 31

Another woman beaten as a child by an alcoholic parent told us she too had vowed "I will never use drugs, I will never live on the streets and I will never prostitute. I used drugs, I lived on the streets and I was a prostitute".

Chloe's Story...

I was in the city, shooting dope, smoking crack. Just got out of rehab, feeling good, no habit yet, ready to party one more time. Well, my usual and "safest spot" didn't have anything. "Wait an hour" they said. Well that wasn't an option. Off I went to check out a few more of my many stomping grounds. I ended up at a dope house I had never been to before. (Me and a guy that was tagging along with me for the free high.) We bought our shit and stayed there for the whole night. By morning my "friend" had left, I was feeling tore up, and starting to really look it too, when in walked one of the most beautiful men I've ever seen. He was tall, about six foot, probably two hundred pounds from what I could see, all muscles. He had beautiful brown eyes and dark skin.

Now being the only white girl in the house, I was really looking for support. Somebody, you know protection, in case one of the girls flipped out on me, or one of the guys decided they wanted to have their way with me. I have always put myself into high risk situations. Sometimes nothing happens, but the other times, well let's just say I wasn't in the mood for that type of confrontation today.

He eyed me, talked to a few people and made his way to me. The eye contact was intense. I also knew he had a pocket full of drugs and a wallet full of money. I was very good at seeing those kinds of things. To move my story along, I never went home. At least not for a couple of weeks. He had a girlfriend, but she was in jail. But that didn't matter, he was falling in love with me. He was my protection on the streets, my dealer. He bought me clothes, got my hair done, gave me a roof over my head, (not always the same one) and he was also my pimp. A whole new world for me. I realize now that I provided the clothes, drugs, food and everything else. I realize now I didn't need him. Think about it, his girlfriend is in jail and he needed another meal ticket. Me. Insane. I felt like life was just running, tricking, and stealing. But we did it with "class." Brand new Cadillac, Timbs, leathers, endless supply of dope.

His girlfriend got out of jail a month after I met him. She quickly took my spot. Nobody ever told her about me. I just fell into my new place. And I really understood my spot. I didn't get new clothes, shoes, drugs all day long. In fact, my licks didn't come to the house anymore, he wanted me to walk the streets. And when I laughed and said "No, what the fuck," I didn't get any more out of my mouth and I felt his hand full fist across my face. I couldn't believe he did that. I thought we had something special. Even if his girlfriend was home, didn't we have an understanding? I know he beats his girls, but wasn't I different? Somebody help me.

Well that next day I walked out of the house, called 911—told them to take me or I'll die by my own hand or someone else's. Thank God, because I have been directed down the road that God wants me on.

Chloe, Age 24

And then there was Janice.

At age twenty-five, I was introduced to freebasing cocaine. At first I would only get a little buzz, but still acted like the same old me—hysterically funny, fun loving and everyone wanted me around. Every party that was thrown I was called upon to join. I was told, it wouldn't be a party without me there—me, the life of the party!

I then became someone different. The more I used, the looser and wilder I got. I also wore a suit of armor. I thought I was invincible.

Years rolled by and at the age of thirty-three the fun was over. I got into trouble facing a state bid with a possession charge. I was no longer free-basing, I was using crack cocaine. I felt my life was over and from this hell, I sunk deeper. I became wide open for anything. I became someone I never thought I could be and I just didn't care about nothing.

I started renting my brand new car out for crack and when that ran out and my car wasn't back, I would hook up with someone and go boosting. I thought I was the best booster around. I would steal anything that dealers would want. I smoked 24/7 and was losing all my muscles and weight. I looked like shit, but I thought I was the bomb. I was out of control, a complete crack monster.

When the stores would close and we would run out of crack, my so-called friends would try to talk me into hustling money in other ways, like prostitution. I swore to myself I would never do that. Unfortunately, eventually I did because Mr. Crack had so much control over my life. I did anything he told me to do.

My heavy drug use with Mr. Crack continued for about eight months until one day I woke up to two undercover officers with a warrant for my arrest. I'm 39 and looking back now, that was the happiest day of my life. I had been saved—saved from my lover—Mr. Crack!

Janice, Age 39

One thing all of these stories showed us was that addiction and all of its consequences left untreated gets worse or progresses. Sharon's story helps to illustrate this.

Sharon's Story…

I started using cocaine when I met my husband. It started with snorting powder on the weekends with friends. We always had a partying kind of lifestyle. We hooked up with some friends who showed us how to "cook" the powder and smoke it. Still, we only did it on the weekends. We still paid bills and went to work every day. Over the years our crack use progressed slowly to every weekend, then three to four times a week. By then I had my two younger boys and they were babies (21 months apart). We bought a house and worked full-time still. The drug use was getting out of hand. I couldn't turn it down and my husband refused to stop bringing it home. I finally kicked him out for self-preservation, knowing it would be very hard to work and take care of two boys and my house on my own.

I stopped doing drugs for a while, maybe eight or nine months; I didn't know where to get any. My husband always got it. Then I started hearing from our "friends" and they encouraged me to come up. I started going up to their house and getting crack maybe one to two times a month. This level of drug use was maintained for several years with no real negative impact. I kind of considered myself an addict, but arrogantly believed I could control it and that there were lines of behavior I would never cross. In the past couple years I met a few local drug dealers who, once hooked up with, made crack one hundred times more accessible. They also kind of preyed on me, knowing I usually had money and no willpower.

Over the years my boys were diagnosed with ADHD and my husband vanished. The stress from my job was getting to me. I had several bad relationships with men and kind of decided Prince Charming wasn't out there and gave up on ever having a relationship which was kind of sad. Not having many friends and no kind of a social life, I took solace in crack more and more because it was, I felt, my only outlet for stress and the only thing that made me feel good.

I spent more and more money on crack, fell behind on bills and the mortgage and was missing more and more time from work. When the "local" dealers came into my life, they would stop by often, eventually hanging out at my house and using my car. This was the point at which I knew I was out of control and doing things that were dangerous and against the law. I couldn't stop and didn't care.

Sharon, Age 40

Many of the group members like Sharon used even when they felt, and perhaps were, out of control and/or were sick of using. My friend, Carol, was one of these women also. She was raised in a middle class home with two parents, both of whom were alcoholic. She came to treatment because she could not take her alcoholic life anymore. She said she was sick and tired of being sick and tired. She came in as a self-referral and her insurance paid most of her bill. She had a job as a teacher where she earned money for the rest of her fees.

At first I thought she was a real snob, "a better than thou person". In Phase II, I learned to accept her and then like her. She was really a lot like me underneath the superficial trappings. She too was full of fear, doubt and insecurity—too much self-doubt and too little self-love. Her story seemed different, but only on the surface. We really identified with each other. She said that her adult daughter had looked in the mirror one day with her and asked, "Do you feel even a little bit bad about what you do?" This penetrated the fog of her using stupor like a piercing arrow. She finally heard what her daughter said to her and called a rehab. She had come a long way by the time I met her. We realized we were different but the same. She wrote poetry too.

MY LOVER MY FRIEND

Immediately I felt the desire for him well up inside of me.
I was burning with desire and engulfed by his warmth.
Wonderful sensations rippled through my body.
My lover, My friend.
My children dislike him.
My husband dislikes him.
They found him distasteful and vulgar.

My lover, My friend.
I found him in good taste.
He comforted me and consoled me.
He brought out the best in me.
My lover, My friend.
My children withdrew from me.
My husband withdrew from me.
They were repulsed when I thought I was at my best.
My lover, My friend.
My friend gave me strength and courage.
My friend gave me energy.
My friend.
My family saw weakness and disgust.

My family saw sickness and a mere skeleton of myself.
My friend.
I found myself spiraling downward.
I'm losing my husband and my family.
I reach for my friend only to find that I am alone.
My betrayer.
My bottle of vodka.

Carol, Age 45

Another professional woman walked a somewhat different path.

Missy's Story…

I awoke to the smell of freshly brewed coffee and a bright yellow beam of sunlight on my face. I hadn't felt this alive in years. In the distance the radio played Leanne Womacks' "I Hope You Dance." I looked up at the ceiling and started to sing "And if you get the chance to sit it out or dance, I hope you dance. Don't let life pass you by."

For years I had washed the pain of loneliness and frustration down with a drink. Powerful, potent, and numbing the liquor of disease was. I sat on a barstool and thought I was living life. Just like Norm on Cheers, the echo of my name would fill the bar when I arrived. Every so-called friend looking for their next drink would smile, laugh and exclaim, "Hey, about time you got here." I always seemed to find the "new kid" and sit next to that person to make myself feel important.

Important! Now there is a word Oh, that was me all right. I was important. The more I drank the more important and less inhibited, I became and the dreaded conversations that would change the world ensued. Honestly, I can't think of one person of stature who made a life-changing decision for the world—or the next door neighbor for that matter—on a barstool. But this would be the conversation that would change the world, as it was that day. Hours of telling people a new way to look at their same old problem would convince them I was the savior of the world. I was cunning like a fox, knowing full well they would not remember the conversation the next day and be so embarrassed that they would tell everyone that I was the smartest and most sincere person they had ever met. They would yell my praise to the heavens and everyone would become my friend. But my only real friends were named Jack Daniel, Jim Beam, Captain Morgan, and last but not least, Mr. Coors.

And what gentlemen they were. They relaxed me with their smooth style, made me feel warm and fuzzy inside, and wham used and abused me. And last but not least, they left me curious as to what adventures had occurred that had not been, at this point, committed to memory. Memory was that illusive state that would give me slight flashbacks about people, places and things. Memories, brought on by the scent of stale cigarettes, would bring a fleeting glimpse of some sexual act only seen in porn movies with me as the star. And each morning I would wake to vomit the absurd acts of the night before. Disgusted, disappointed and cheap were accolades I gave myself.

But now without liquor, life was better and I could control my behavior. I lie there on the bed with my eyes closed drinking in the smells and listening to the sounds of this new day. Sobriety had brought me to this point of appreciating life. As I open my eyes I look up to see the vision of this glorious day.

Peace filled my being and I smile, happy to be alive and glad to be me.

Missy, Age 38

TERMINATION OF TREATMENT

I had listened while others completed treatment after months of abstinence. All throughout treatment there had been a yearning within me to be where they were. And finally I was.

It had come time for me to complete treatment. I had finished what I had been sent to accomplish. Now it was time to practice applying what I had learned. I had great hopes from my treatment—I was sober and I had learned about the tools to maintain this. I knew what to do and how to do it. I just had to do it. I knew I had to do it even though not everyone was on a straight course to lifelong sobriety. As a matter of fact, many would not make it outside of rehab.

It was clear from the word that reached back to us that some of the folks I had met in my journey were not doing well. One woman had written to say that when she left treatment, she had been sure she would never use again nor go to prison again. Three months later she relapsed and was arrested for possession. This violated her parole and she went back to prison. Another former client indicated that she had been abstinent for several months before she relapsed and went back to prostitution to support her habit. She wrote us after she returned to rehab through drug court.

Not all relapsed, however.

Tanya's Story…

Recovery is a process. Everyday is a struggle but then on the other hand it's also learning something new. I've been clean for a year and it feels great. I'm a whole different daughter and mother and thinking a lot clearer. I'm really proud of my recovery. I wouldn't trade the feeling for anything in the world. It feels like a big accomplishment and goal I've always wanted. To take it day by day and deal with the things on that day. (Actually, sometimes minute by minute.) I try not to look too far ahead. I am a lot happier person. Recovery is like everything to me because without it

I wouldn't be who I am today. I also pray to Allah for giving me the strength to stay strong.

Tanya, Age 35

And still another indicated:

Justine's Story…

Living life clean is a lot better than living it using. I am accomplishing a lot in my life today. When I was using I didn't accomplish nothing but getting high. I still have everyday problems but I don't get high over them and I try not to overreact to them. I just tell myself that it could be worse and I try to talk to someone who's dealt with what I'm going through. I actually have a couple of real friends that love me for me whether I'm happy, sad, mad, or whatever. When I was using I had "friends" that just wanted my dope or a piece of butt and then were gone. I can actually go out today and have fun just going for a walk and acting goofy. I like life in recovery today and I love myself today. Hopefully, I'll never go back to using 'cause I love life clean.

Justine, Age 20

Julia's Story…

I have spent the last eight months attempting to put my alcoholic lifestyle behind me. This is not an easy task for someone who has been either drunk or high, or both for the past seven years. The decision to quit didn't come from some life-changing revelation or even because I had finally gotten myself into enough trouble. I quit when I had the first inkling that I was pregnant.

I didn't just one day decide to become an alcoholic. Just about every member of my family is an alcoholic. So my drinking wasn't shunned. I was welcomed into the fold. My alcoholism was allowed to blossom. I received my first DWI in June of last year. The few sober family members that I do have were shocked and disappointed. So consequently I avoided them. My coworkers were concerned that I might have a problem and allowed me to stay at work each night until after the bars closed. I felt very ashamed of myself and grew even more depressed and withdrawn. Getting drunk in a bar was my only source of fun and amusement. Because I was drunk all of the time, I didn't have feelings and emotions like sober people do. I felt stronger and more at ease when I was drunk. But alcohol seriously impaired my judgment. The same year I received my second DWI. My car was impounded and I went to jail. Thankfully, a friend bailed me out the next morning.

In September I met my boyfriend. My life began to change. He was someone that I could spend time with and have fun with without being drunk. We moved in together in December. By the end of January I realized that I was pregnant. That was the push I needed to quit drinking and using drugs. I realized that I wanted a healthy baby. My life wasn't just about me anymore. I had a lot of love in my life that I didn't want to lose by drinking. I slowly began to climb out of the hole of depression and drug abuse that I had dug myself into. For the first time in years I was actually happy with my life.

I have a lot of people supporting me in my sober life that I wouldn't have if I was still using. I get plenty of support through GCASA and don't regret for a moment my eight months of sobriety. More importantly, I feel better about my life and myself.

Julia, Age 26

When I asked my counselor about recovery versus relapse, she said that success rates vary and are reported differently by different authorities. I learned that recovery can never be taken for granted—the results are individual and unpredictable.

They told us in group that some authorities say one out of seven abstainers maintain abstinence. Others use a model which indicates that 1/3 of all who try will not relapse, 1/3 will relapse with an ultimate return to recovery, and the remaining 1/3 will never gain straight-line sobriety. There are still others who report that 4 out of 7 people completing treatment will stay sober.

Who knew for sure? I just knew I did not plan to relapse again mostly because I realized I was no longer alone. I could ask for help. I had sober support, especially from my friends from treatment and AA/NA. I had a higher power and a sponsor. And I was at long last going to be off probation with a chance for a driver's license in the distance. We will see what tomorrow brings.

THE END FOR NOW...

APPENDIX A

MOTHERS AND MOTHERING

A Hallmark Mother:

Special Need

Sometimes you need someone
who'll listen,
Sometimes you need someone
who'll smile,
Sometimes you need someone
who cares about you
to just be around for a while.
Sometimes you need someone
who'll help you,
Sometimes you need someone
who'll share,
And those are the times
when you can depend
on a mother to always be there

Karen Ravn (5)

An Addict Mother:
The consequences of substance abuse for women are profound in role function-
ing and the ability to contribute to society and the well-being of their children
and family. (15)

Some Mothers Were Remembered as Addicts...

My Mother
"Martha Stewart mom..."

*My mother and I were very close, long talks. She was very loving, understanding,
cooked dinner, cleaned the house, and baked cookies. She was there when I hurt
myself, when I got my period, and when I got my first kiss. She stuck up for me when
her boyfriend molested me and she found out. I'm sure I was her favorite. She loved
me so much and I her. We went everywhere together.*

"Mommy Dearest mom..."

*She dragged me into her alcoholism, called me names, woke me up in the middle of
the night and kept me up to cry and dump on me. Threw me down some stairs, sat on
my chest and I almost passed out. Moved me out of house and didn't tell me or the
people I was coming. Dragged me by my hair, put me in charge of raising her children, spent all my money at the bar. Kept me from my father. Slept with my boyfriend
'cuz I was still a virgin. Moved him in with her.*

*I don't like my mom right now. She has never said I'm sorry for anything. She just
told my younger brother and sister that she fucked up my life and wouldn't do it to
them. I want to hear it from her.*

*She'll get hers 'cuz she has emphysema and I don't care. I'm not sure I have any
love for her.*

Gloria, Age 44

I was such a young girl watching you lay on your bed without clothes. Most of the time you were in your own world. I didn't feel important to you. I saw you with women, you even let one touch me and abuse my brother and I. Like it didn't matter, 'cause she meant more to you. You came off so weak, you didn't want to face reality. You did love us, but never knew how to show it. Even when you had a chance to fight for us, you never did up until the day you died. You were hopeless throughout your life! You failed me mom, time after time.

Suzanne, Age 29

At fifteen, nearing the end of my residency at a group home for children, I recall one of the last letters she wrote me. It included something like, "I met this guy you'll really like. He's cute and he's in a band. I can't wait to introduce you!" When I finally went home, I thought, "How great it is to have this cool mom to party with!" No rules, endless partying, nothing to hide.

A short time passed though and this woman, who in my mind was my mother and my friend, brought me shame. My mind battled between those invisible lines of mother or friend. Hanging out with her and other friends, friends older than me, younger than her, gave me no distinguishable line between what was mother, what was friend. Her behavior disgusted me at times, when she openly cheated on my father. At times her behavior gave me a strong sense that I needed to take care of her when I rubbed her back while she was drunk and puking. Somehow though, I was always loyal to her. That one moment in time when she failed me the most will forever make me angry at her selfishness. I walked in the rain to our friend's house where she was partying, crying, razorblade in hand, and when a "friend" answered the door, he said, "No she's not here." I saw her run and hide. She never came to see me at the hospital. With no rules my friend, Mom, enabled that cute boy in a band and I to become parents at sixteen. My mother at that time, in my eyes, failed me. I will never forgive her selfishness. She's sober now, the damage done. I'm all grown up. I should add, though, some part of me thinks she did the best she could.

Sally, Age 27

At the starting of the week
you give us the love we often seek
you kiss the wounds of your weekend war
and would think our hearts not sore
Tuesday comes, you seem distracted

sorry for the way you acted
stricken with guilt and shame
you take us to the toy store for a brand new game
know that you'll be stopping
for your case of beer
and even dolls and games
cannot calm my fear
By Wednesday we can't wake you
he hit you pretty hard
your clothes dirty, bloody
my brain is so scarred
Thursday is a blackout
for you and for me
I realized early on, this isn't for a child's eyes to see
Friday gets real bad
too painful to recall
makes me feel so sad
makes me feel so small
never sleep on Saturday
I hear screams, banging, glass
I PRAY
Sunday is dismal, calm, quiet
we're all tired from the riot
Sarah and I play with dolls while
you sleep off the alcohol
Tomorrow you'll be ready to give us that
day of love for which I pray

Kelly, Age 23

Some remembered mothers who suffered in other ways...

I remember when she was 46 and I was 10...

I wish everyone would just be quiet! Don't they see what is happening? She's in the basement again. I will go down in a minute. Will she really go? How could she go and just leave me here with these people. Why can't they see what I see. Why am I the only one who sees her pain. I will go talk to her and tell her everything will be okay. I'll just make everybody laugh and clean the kitchen extra good tonight and everything will be okay. At least for today. If I can just get her to stay home today—then she'll see that things are okay. If I can take it, why can't she. It's not so bad that she has to leave, is it? Why won't she tell me anything. And when she cries why doesn't she know that there's nothing I can do about it—What makes her this way? If I can take it—why can't she.

She is 76 and I'm now 40. Dad is dead...

She belongs to me now. We are safe. No one can hurt us anymore. We have coffee and talk about the news. We look out the window. Bluebirds, cardinals, a light snow-fall. We waited a long time but we have peace now. Too much peace for both of us sometimes. She's lonely without dad—but she doesn't miss everybody else. All that matters is that I have her all to myself now. If she could only hold on a little longer. Then she can go where she wants to go. To be with dad. She stayed for me you know. She remembers the basement. We mangled clothes and cried together. She remembered. She knew I was there. I was never sure if she even knew I was there. I'm here now with her drinking coffee, sneaking cigarettes, and watching the birds out the window. Quiet. We like it quiet.

My mother was not a big drinker. Actually growing up I don't remember anyone in my family drinking or drugging around me.

Sharon, Age 41

My parents got divorced when I was five, and from then on I basically grew up with the babysitters. She had to work two or three jobs at a time to be able to support me and my three siblings.

Growing up I had no discipline. Once we were old enough, the babysitter was gone and we made all our own choices. I would go to school whenever I wanted; leave early and she'd always write me the excuse the next day.

At fourteen, we'd have parties when my mom was working nights. She'd find out, but there was never any real consequence afterwards.

As I look back now, I wish so much that she had told me no or actually grounded me <u>once</u> in my life. I have grown up thinking I can do whatever I want, without consequence, and have found out that in the real world, that doesn't work. I also find that I have a very hard time disciplining my own children.

Today I am just trying to use my own power to push myself. I am actually doing quite well, and I'm finding out that with some self-discipline I'm actually getting something out of life.

Diane, Age 23

My mother was a person who tried to protect me from my father. I remember seeing my mom get beat and hurt so much and she drank a lot. My mother was a sick person and I was the only one who took care of her. She was 49 when she died in 2002 and that hurt because when she died she died with two years clean. My mom was an only child. She had no brothers or sisters so it must have been hard for her when she was growing up. She also had a son. His name is Joseph and she gave him up for adoption so she wouldn't lose me. Life just wasn't good for my mom. She would always get into bad relationships and she just didn't deserve to get beat all the time. I love my mom and she loved me. She only did her best for me and I'm thankful for that.

Jaime, Age 29

My mother was a mother of eight children. She was married to my dad, an alcoholic. She did everything he said and that's just how it was back then. I don't remember her hugging me. I guess our family was just not very love-showing. I guess my mother was passive in everything that happened. School was hard for me because I couldn't get any help at home. Mom with all of us, and dad drinking all day. Then I discovered I didn't have to go to school at about fourteen or fifteen. I would get the younger ones off to school. That would keep dad happy while mom worked. Wow! So now I'm actually raising my two younger brothers and sister. Well my mother just went with the flow of things at home. If she didn't I'd know it because she'd have a black eye or some kind of proof to show it. She didn't protect us or it would be her. I can remember mom and dad going somewhere and I told them I wasn't raising their kids. My dad broke my nose and my mom didn't say or do anything except the next day she did write me a note to go to the hospital. She tried. Well, now I'm grown up. I see that she wasn't the best of moms but also now I understand. I just wish I understood then. I'm glad I still have her now, and better!

Julia, Age 39

Some remembered mothers who died young…

Mom,

I grew up knowing you till I was twelve, but it wasn't long enough because I don't have any real memories of you. There are a couple times that stick out in my head but I'd rather not remember you that way. Like our last family vacation to the West Coast and you were so sick but you still wanted to do everything and see everything. You were so weak and I was mad because you would get tired and not do all the things I wanted to do only the things you wanted to do. Now I see why, because it was your last chance on this earth to see them. As I look back on it now, you were the strongest woman I ever met. Everyone tells me how I look just like you or Grandma will say you act the same way your mother did and even if she's referring to it as a bad thing, it still makes me proud, because I want to be just like you. You were strong, independent, smart, beautiful (inside and out), and happy (even with all your struggles, you made the best out of what life offered you.) These are the characteristics I cherish in you and I try to model in my own life.

Anne, Age 23

So many memories, yet not so clear anymore. Memories of the woman I called mom. I can remember this beautiful woman with long red hair and eyes to match the bluest sea. She was strong, loving, and full of life. She was everything I wish I could be. All this anger builds up inside me because our time was cut too short. I lay awake many nights wondering what my life would be like if she were still here. I still remember her laugh; contagious and giddy. I remember the way it felt when she would comfort me when I was ill. Her hands softly rubbing my head to ease the pain. How I long for that feeling again. The memory of her fades and fades away. Yet each day that passes I still remember that beautiful woman with long red hair and eyes to match the bluest ocean.

Juliet, Age 22

At age fifteen my mother died. She was my foundation, which also could be considered the roots of my existence. She was not like anyone else's mother. She made me. My mother taught me to be curious, to be proud of tackling new experiences rather than taking comfort in the safety of following others. She introduced me to the raspy voice of Marianne Faithfull, the beautiful prose of Anne Sexton and the hospitality of the South. She taught me to delight in what was unique about me, and for all that and so much more I'll always be grateful.

After my mother's passing, I was crazy, uncontrollable and ticking like a small bomb. My grades fell from A's and B's to C's and D's. I was in trouble all the time. If I made it to school I spent a fair amount of the time in detention. Two months later, I received my driver's license which equated to freedom in my young mind. I was a raw nerve and felt I had no skin. There was something missing in my life and my mission was to find it or at least find an adequate substitute. My quest was completed when I found it...Heroin.

This is where I worry I sound like a Census Bureau statistic or some sort of case study. This is where the psychotherapist and counselors chime in and inform me about their psychoanalytic theories of my life. That is when I respond to them, "I knew exactly what I was doing." In all actuality, I had no idea what I was doing or how I was going to get myself out of it. I was just another teenage girl gone wrong.

As a suburban, naïve sixteen-year old girl, I ventured into that dirty and corrupted city and met some individuals who introduced me to this morally deteriorated and sordid culture, which I never deemed existed in such a city. They used me as I used them. I began to withdraw into myself, away from the laughable noise of my friends. Focusing instead on the sensation of addiction, the lovely spinning feeling in my head, the way I would veer in and out of conversations. With my pinpoint pupils and my newly imbalanced chemistry it made me feel like the walls were tilting and the floor undulating beneath my feet.

So my little dark and dank downward spiral is in remission as of this moment. I try not to think too much about it. It has been years of active addiction or dull and insipid institutional existence. My grief (and addiction) does not go away. It lives an ever-changing life of its own within mine. Yet for all the absurdity of having my mother missing from my life, her death left me with a perspective I am grateful to have: Any moment could be my last. It's important to treat one another with appropriate respect, humor, and gratitude. Her legacy guides me. I look for her. I look for that indescribable mood and the feeling that is hallowed splendor. And I see her in bits and slivers, like light streaming through chinks in the dense forest, in instances that surprise me as beautiful, in things obviously radiant and mysterious as was she.

Will I ever get her back? No. Just like the tree, you can replant another and hope it grows new. Yet, the utterly inconceivable fact is there is no adequate replacement for it. That disorientated feeling returns over and over again. I must relearn at a million different moments that she should be here but is gone. And no matter how many chemicals I use to paint or sandblast my brain, I know by now, only too well, that you can never substitute a mother's love. As you can never restore a fallen tree to it's original home ground.

Christine, Age 25

And some mothers were remembered lovingly...

Dear Mom,

I'm writing you a letter to tell you how much I appreciate your character. You're loving, caring, and nurturing. And you're always there for me. You take me to all my doctor's appointments and listen to my baby's heartbeat. It's a beautiful thing to be able to share that with one another.

You are at my house every afternoon at 1:00 pm on Tuesdays waiting to go to drug court. You've been to every date with me for a whole year. No one else had their mother or even their father, family or a friend go with them the whole time. I really appreciate that. These are just two of the things I'm thankful for having you as my mother. Thank you.

Kay, Age 19

My mother was a stay at home mom. She didn't work outside the home. She had seven children; five girls and two boys. My mom did what she was told to do. She raised her voice all the time. For the longest time I didn't like my mother 'cause she said something to me when I was around twelve years old and didn't remember saying it. (I don't love you. I hate you.) My mom was there when I've needed mom to be there. Down the road my mom asked me why I didn't come to see her when my dad was not living home ('cause of illness) and I confronted her and said, well when I was twelve years old you said something to me and she asked what and I told her and she said I don't remember saying that. She apologized to me and ever since we have been close. I love my mom.

Cathy, Age 31

My mother was a very irresponsible person. I felt like I was never loved all my life. Things happened to me as a child and she never had my back as a child. I was always in the wrong. I could never be right about anything. But as I got older we started having better conversations. She's been a better listener and gives me advice on things, but it wasn't until my father passed away that we started getting closer. She now treats me like a human being. And I can talk to her about anything. I finally have a mom that I never had.

Sandy, Age 46

My mother is like most mothers. She carried me for nine months; she cares about me; she worries about me, but like some mothers she was very verbally and physically abusive toward me. But one day that changed. I'm not sure what it took to keep her from abusing me, but she stopped. About a year ago my mother realized I was a different person. She figured out that I was getting high, not going to work, not taking care of myself; I didn't care what people thought or how they looked at me. It was my life and I was going to do what I wanted. Until one night when I went over to my mother's house, took some of her pills, then the next day I was on my way to a friend's house and the police pulled me over. Not knowing what was going on I thought they had pulled me over for speeding until the officer came to the window and told me to step out of the car. When I did, they handcuffed me and told me I was under arrest. It wasn't until I was back at the police station that I found out why. My mother had me arrested for taking her pills. And, of course, I was pissed, but while I was in jail I realized why she did it. She did it because she was worried, and going to jail was the kick in the ass I needed to get me here.

Bonita, Age 22

But all were surely remembered...

Myself as a Mother

I am a mother...good, bad or indifferent; I am a mother. As I'm walking through the grocery store with my children, an older woman stops me to compliment the behavior of my nine year old son, "He is so polite" she said, with a tone of surprise in her voice. A gentleman told me how "well-mannered" my boy is.

I've made mistakes while raising him. I've put him into some very unsafe predicaments. On the other hand I've always been as protective over him as a wolf with her pups. I never did teach him responsibility. I guess that's because I wasn't being respon-

sible myself. I used and sold drugs in his presence. I took him places, he never should have been and showed him things he never should have seen. He still loves me and I love him. Through all of it, I managed to teach him honesty and respect.

I can't think of much else good that I've done for him. He's emotionally and mentally disturbed because of me—his mother and his protector. He still wants to give me a chance, and I'm thankful for that. I am learning to be a better role model for my son and his new sister.

Martha, Age 34

It's been three years now since the day I became so wrapped up in myself and my addiction, that I made the decision to stop being a mother.

At seventeen, when I became a mother to my daughter, I did well. I was an excellent caretaker and kept my daughter clean and fed and on a routine no matter what. I worked hard at a full-time job to provide for us. For about two years I felt I was everything a child needs. Then I grew up.

I realized I was in a bad relationship with her father. He was abusive. If I left it would mean we'd have to live with my alcoholic parents. I felt we were safer with her father, but the abuse continued. I started drinking and using, and my mothering skills slowly deteriorated. I no longer had a routine for her or myself; I missed a lot of work. I left her with her father for days at a time.

I felt like I missed out on my teenage years and I was desperately trying to get it back, in all the wrong ways, at all the wrong times. My daughter's life was suddenly filled with the chaos, fighting and pain, I swore I'd never cast upon my own children.

We moved back to my parents. A big blur of two years passed. Drinking and using drugs with my parents, my brother and daughter innocently remained in our care. I had different men, went back to her father on and off. I'd leave her with my parents. My use became out of control. I got a DWI, lost my car, my job and my mind. Her father took her and I used SO much and ran away.

Two more years of a blur. I'm all those things an addicted mother is. I am an addict and that is why I have done what I've done.

Seven months clean now. She is six. I want to be her caretaker. I want to give her security, a routine, and love. She knows I'm here and I love her for now. Our visitations are healing our hearts little by little. God will guide us through this, and what happens will be right.

Jeanne, Age 24

There is one thing I can say about myself as an addict and mother. I never used around my son, but my son was not getting my full attention. I would pick him up tired...let's go a step further, <u>exhausted!</u>

There were times when I sat down on the couch and fell asleep. My son had the whole house to himself (there are still several c.d.'s that I cannot find.) He would want to play or go to the park and mommy was just too tired. If I would go somewhere with him it was just for a short period of time because I wanted to relax.

The first day of my days with my son were a disaster, and I know that he knew I wasn't myself.

I'm so glad that those days are over. My time today is priceless with my precious son!

Lisa, Age 22

***How I see myself as a mother when I was using**: I was a very irresponsible, self-centered and I felt like I didn't have a care in the world. But under all that drug use I was in pain. A lot of pain.*

***How I see myself today**: I've lost some years but it's never too late to start again. I see myself today as a single parent. I see myself as an understanding, compassionate person, loving and caring about human beings that myself and my ex brought into the world.*

I sometimes have a hard time, but God manages to help me out. I do what is best for my children. I love them with all my heart and soul, and as long as I stay strong they will always have a mother who will be understanding, loving and caring. And that is the way they know me, as Real Mom.

Amy, Age 39

I had my first baby when I was sixteen and was an all right mom. But I had a lot of trouble trying to raise a baby when I was still a child myself so that's where the grandparents came in. Then I waited a few years and had my other two children. Their father was a drinker and partied, so I started using crack. It was hard to be patient with the kids when I was partying myself. My behavior as a mother while I was using was not anything I would want any child to go through! I left their dad and was with someone who was a nut case. I know now 'cause I can see clearly.

But anyway back to me being the mother. I wasn't much of one. I would rush to feed them or bath them just to get back to getting high. No quality time spent. My daughter was in kindergarten and half the time I didn't even get her up for school and she didn't go. She had to do it all over again because of me and she remembers and tells me that too. I also got to the point where I'd leave them upstairs all day to "play" so I had the downstairs for me and "my friends" to get high. I would take food up to them. Even on nice days if they went out, I was always yelling at them for nothing. Now I see that. I was a yeller. I wasn't interested in anything they said to me. I guess you could say I just had them there and as long as they didn't bother me I was all right. Now they've taken my new babies away, I've stopped all the crazy stuff and I'm more patient and loving. When you're high you have no emotions and now I'm not getting high. I have all my emotions back. I like feeling love for all my children. I like being a good mother. I look back and see how I treated my children and I would never want any child to go through that. They will remember and I just hope my children will forgive me.

Holly, Age 27

Before I began getting too deep into my addiction I felt I was a very mature young adult who could nurture a child. I felt I was responsible enough to bring up a child and teach values to him or her. I was always available to my children. I would be loving and understanding. I would try to keep my children safe as possible. I always provided the best for them when I could. I always thought I was a good mother and wife. Getting them off to school, helping them with their homework, and making sure dinner was on the table. Then the time came when the drugs and the partying progressed in my life and it was more important. I chose that over my children. I began to become a mother who started isolating herself away from her children. I was preoccupied with other things, people, and places. I became what I did not intend to be. Destructive to myself and to others, especially to my children. I became very self-centered. I was spending all the money, having no values, and I became very irresponsible at the end.

Helen, Age 40

It goes without saying that I wasn't being a very good mother to my boys. With their ADHD they were always difficult and had a lot of behavioral and emotional problems. When I neglected them they went out of control, but again, I didn't care.

I finally lost my job (which was a long time coming). Three weeks later I got my retirement money and was also getting unemployment. I went through about five thousand dollars for crack in about six weeks. I had no feelings, no sense, no caution. I didn't think about anything but crack. I couldn't even be sad or remorseful for what I *was doing to my children or family who at this point (probably way before) suspected something was seriously wrong. Of course I spent every penny in my bank account and my unemployment was stopped. I finally came to a screeching halt. A "friend" totaled my car. I was left with <u>nothing</u>. Didn't even know how I would feed us or explain <u>everything</u> to my family.*

I ended up at the Department of Social Services and told them <u>everything</u>. They have been very kind and helpful. For the first time in years I'm getting treatment for my addiction and getting back to a somewhat normal life (be that as it may). I still worry about possible repercussions. Loss of self-esteem, independence, and respect. I'm concentrating on my kids and myself and trying not to worry about the rest. I'm hoping to get back all that I lost even my self-respect and independence.

Lori, Age 39

When I was asked "What do you want to be when you grow up?" I always answered a "stay at home" mom. Partly because my mom wasn't and also because I enjoyed kids.

When I did become a mother I was still working and it was difficult. I eased that difficulty with pot to escape the overloading stress of being a working mom. After my second child was born, I didn't have to work anymore. It was great! I took them to the park, the library, and many other activities. My husband and I would have picnics with the kids on weekends or we would go visit family or to the local beach together as a family. I was getting what I had always wanted.

In 2001 everything changed. My husband died suddenly and unexpectedly. I was overwhelmed with shock, grief and depression. I was now a <u>single mother</u> and was lost. I couldn't or didn't know how to cope.

I turned to drinking and drugs. There I didn't have to deal with my sadness and anger. I became detached from mourning him—it was too hard!

In that process I pushed my kids away and partying became first and foremost. I became moody with the kids. They weren't sure what "mom" they were coming home to. I would lie to get them out of the house so I could party. I would get short with them if I couldn't get my drugs. I was just plain unreliable and it was unsafe for them.

Now I am working on me for them. For them to have the mom they deserve to have—a dependable drug-free mom.

Donna, Age 33

First I would like to say that I love my two children with all my heart. The current situation with them not living with me has left me with a lot of turmoil, grief, and tears. With that said, I feel that most of that grief and turmoil has been caused by my alcoholism. I let them down. They were not always safe in my care because of my drinking. My daughter has seen the effects of my destructive behavior with my two short trips to jail for DWI, lost jobs, and lost pride. I have not been there in many ways that I should have been. My mother never wanted to be touched, physical affection I guess I would put it. Therefore, I think that is why it's so hard for me to give hugs and stuff too. I recognize it, it hurts, but I find it hard to change. I resist change somehow. My goal is to stay in sobriety and work through some of these things so I will be a better mother in the future. But I have to want it more than anything else. All I know right now is that this addiction and everything that bothers me inside consciously or unconsciously is slowly eating me alive.

Mae, Age 34

I'm a mother of two kids who started out as a mother who was faithful in having kids at first. Then when I had to be alone with my kids without the father, I started to be an angry and unloving person 'cause I wanted to party like the father was. So I wanted to be a little like my mother who was always there for me without my father being in our life. But just because I wanted a family with a house and wanted to do things together like some families do, does not mean it would be that way. Especially if you start something that you think you have control over like drinking and drugs. So for me I lost myself and didn't care about anything and anybody.

And then I came into a program that helped me learn to help myself and learn how to help others too, and everything began to change. Today I am learning how to forgive myself for the past, but not to forget it. The program has helped me to go on with my life, to do it one day at a time and to the best of my ability.

Vicki, Age 24

APPENDIX B

NOTES

Intimate Relationships

From adolescence to old age, girls and women's use of drugs and alcohol are influenced by the relationships in their lives. Adolescent girls appear to be more vulnerable to peer pressure compared to boys and may experiment with drugs and alcohol in order to feel accepted by peers. Female addicts and alcoholics also are more likely to have a substance-abusing partner than are male addicts and alcoholics. It is estimated that one-third to one-half of women with addictions are living with a man who also is addicted to drugs or alcohol. Women who are married to men who drink heavily also are likely to abuse alcohol. Over half of the adult women admitted to Caron Foundation for treatment in 2001 were married.

Young women tend to be introduced to drugs and alcohol by older men with whom they are intimately involved. At the Caron Foundation, approximately 25% of heroin-addicted female patients have been introduced to heroin by their intimate partners compared to less than 5% of the male patients. Female heroin-addicted patients also were more likely to be introduced to heroin by an opposite-sex friend compared to male patients who were more likely to be introduced to the drug by a same-sex friend or acquaintance.

Likewise, the female patients were more likely to receive money to buy heroin and to support their drug habit from their partners than were the male patients. The women also were more likely to share needles with their partner than were men. Other research also indicates that intravenous (IV) drug-using women are likely to have sexual activity with IV-drug using men. These findings have important implications about women's vulnerability to drug use. Women tend to be introduced to drugs and alcohol through intimate relationships which can have potentially disastrous health consequences for women. (20)

Relapse

Relapse is a process. A process is an ongoing situation that can be interrupted or changed at any time rather that a static event that is over and cannot be changed.

The process of relapse occurs within the patient. Relapse patterns are formed by attitudes, values, and behavioral responses that occur inside the patient.

Relapse manifests itself in a progressive pattern of behavior. It keeps getting worse until the process is interrupted or changed.

The relapse dynamic allows the symptoms of an illness to become reactivated or causes other debilitating symptoms. The process of uninterrupted relapse can result in the onset or recurrence of symptoms that have been arrested or can result in other related symptoms. To arrest the symptoms of a disease is to control or manage it rather than to cure it. (11)

Inpatient Services

Inpatient programs supply a safe and efficient setting to provide intensive evaluation, treatment and rehabilitation services which consist of medically-supervised, twenty-four hour a day, seven days per week care for persons suffering from chemical dependence.

Inpatient services include intensive management of chemical dependence symptoms in addition to medical management and/or monitoring of physical or mental complications from substance use.

Included in the category of Inpatient Services are the thirteen OASAS-operated Addiction Treatment Centers (ATCs) located throughout New York State. Each center provides a wide range of quality programs to addicted persons and their families in a cost-efficient and effective manner.(13)

Hiv+ Prevelance Among Women

A decade ago women seemed to be on the periphery of the epidemic, today they are at the epicentre.

55% of all HIV+ adults in Sub-Saharan Africa are women (UNAIDS 2000).

A rise in infection among women is apparent even in countries which initially reported epidemics among men who have sex with men and intravenous drug users.

Some sample statistics:

- Today 47 percent of the 36.1 million people living with HIV are women and this proportion is growing

- Of the 16,000 new infections that occur everyday, up to sixty percent are now amongst women (ILO)

- Women now account for 52 percent of the 17.5 million adults who have died from the disease since the epidemic began (UNAIDS)

- Since the beginning of the epidemic, over nine million women have died from HIV/AIDS—related illnesses (17)

Fetal Alcohol Syndrome

Alcohol is the active drug in beer, wine, and liquor.

A twelve-ounce glass of beer has about the same amount of alcohol as a glass of wine or a shot of liquor. Many drug store medicines also contain alcohol.

Any amount of alcohol drunk by a pregnant woman reaches her fetus within minutes and stays there up to twenty-four hours.

Fetal Alcohol Syndrome (FAS) happens when alcohol drunk by a woman who is pregnant affects her developing fetus. (A fetus is what the baby is called when it is growing inside its mother.) FAS problems may include:

- deformed face, teeth, and head shape

- malformed organs inside the body

- deformed heart

- problems when growing

- low intelligence and retardation

- problems seeing

- problems hearing

- trouble concentrating

- trouble learning and remembering things

FAS is a major birth defect in the United States. More than forty thousand FAS babies are born in the United States each year. About one in 750 births per year in the United States is a full-blown case of FAS. That's about five thousand FAS babies each year. (In order to qualify as full blown FAS, three conditions must exist: delayed intellectual development; slowed growth during pregnancy and after birth; and facial abnormalities.) About thirty-five thousand babies are born in the United States with other Fetal Alcohol Effects. World figures are not now available on FAS.

FAS babies require extra care when young and extra medical and school attention as they grow.

No one knows how much alcohol causes FAS.

FAS can be prevented if a woman doesn't drink alcohol at all while pregnant, or when she is trying to become pregnant, or if she thinks she might be pregnant.

Some teenage women who drink alcohol may become pregnant too, and must be aware of the risks of FAS.

A pregnant woman who can't stop drinking even when she knows it might cause FAS may be alcoholic. She can find help by contacting an alcoholism treatment center or Alcoholics Anonymous. Their numbers are in a telephone book. (10)

The Twelve Steps

Step One
"We admitted we were powerless over alcohol—that our lives had become unmanageable."
Who cares to admit complete defeat? Admission of powerlessness is the first step in liberation. Relation of humility to sobriety. Mental obsession plus physical allergy. Why must every A.A. hit bottom?

Step Two
"Came to believe that a Power greater than ourselves could restore us to sanity."
What can we believe in? A.A. does not demand belief; Twelve Steps are only suggestions. Importance of an open mind. Variety of ways to faith. Substitution of A.A. as Higher Power. Plight of the disillusioned. Roadblocks of indifference and prejudice. Lost faith found in A.A. Problems of intellectuality and self-sufficiency. Negative and positive thinking. Self-righteousness. Defiance is an outstanding characteristic of alcoholics. Step Two is a rallying point to sanity. Right relation to God.

Step Three
"Made a decision to turn our will and our lives over to the care of God <u>as we under-stood Him.</u>"
Step Three is like opening of a locked door. How shall we let God into our lives? Willingness is the key. Dependence as a means to independence. Dangers of self-sufficiency. Turning our will over to Higher Power. Misuse of will-power. Sustained and personal exertion necessary to conform to God's will.

Step Four
"Made a searching and fearless moral inventory of ourselves."
How instincts can exceed their proper function. Step Four is an effort to discover our liabilities. Basic problem of extremes in instinctive drives. Misguided moral inventory can result in guilt, grandiosity, or blaming others. Assets can be noted with liabilities. Self-justification is dangerous. Willingness to take inventory brings light and new confidence. Step Four is beginning of lifetime practice. Common symptoms of emotional insecurity are worry, anger, self-pity, and depression. Inventory reviews relationships. Importance of thoroughness.

Step Five
"Admitted to God, to ourselves, and to another human being the exact nature of our wrongs."
Twelve Steps deflate ego. Step Five is difficult but necessary to sobriety and peace of mind. Confession is an ancient discipline. Without fearless admission of defects, few could stay sober. What do we receive from Step Five? Beginning of true kinship with man and God. Lose sense of isolation, receive forgiveness and give it; learn humility; gain honesty and realism about ourselves. Necessity for complete honesty. Danger of rationalization. How to choose the person in whom to confide. Results are tranquility and consciousness of God. Oneness with God and man prepares us for following Steps.

Step Six
"Were entirely ready to have God remove all these defects of character."
Step Six necessary to spiritual growth. The beginning of a lifetime job. Recognition of difference between striving for objective—and perfection. Why we must keep trying. "Being ready" is all-important. Necessity of taking action. Delay is dangerous. Rebellion may be fatal. Point at which we abandon limited objectives and move toward God's will for us.

Step Seven
"Humbly asked Him to remove our shortcomings."
What is humility? What can it mean to us? The avenue to true freedom of the human spirit. Necessary aid to survival. Value of ego puncturing. Failure and misery transformed by humility. Strength from weakness. Pain is the admission price to new life. Self-centered fear chief activator of defects. Step Seven is change in attitude which permits us to move out of ourselves toward God.

Step Eight
"Made a list of all persons we had harmed, and became willing to make amends to them all."
This and the next two Steps are concerned with personal relations. Learning to live with others is a fascinating adventure. Obstacles: reluctance to forgive; non-admission of wrongs to others; purposeful forgetting. Necessity of exhaustive survey of past. Deepening insight results from thoroughness. Kinds of harm done to others. Avoiding extreme judgments. Taking the objective view. Step Eight is the beginning of the end of isolation.

Step Nine
"Made direct amends to such people wherever possible, except when to do so would injure them or others."
A tranquil mind is the first requisite for good judgment. Good timing is important in making amends. What is courage? Prudence means taking calculated chances. Amends begin when we join A.A. Peace of mind cannot be bought at the expense of others. Need for discretion. Readiness to take consequences of our past and to take responsibility for well-being of others is spirit of Step Nine.

Step Ten
"Continued to take personal inventory and when we were wrong promptly admitted it."
Can we stay sober and keep emotional balance under all conditions? Self-searching becomes a regular habit. Admit, accept, and patiently correct defects. Emotional hangover. When past is settled with, present challenges can be met. Varieties of inventory. Anger, resentments, jealousy, envy, self-pity, hurt pride—all led to the bottle. Self-restraint first objective. Insurance against "big-shot-ism." Let's look at credits as well as debits. Examination of motives.

Step Eleven

"Sought through prayer and meditation to improve our conscious contact with God <u>as we understood Him,</u> praying only for knowledge of His will for us and the power to carry that out."

Meditation and prayer main channels to Higher Power. Connection between self-examination and meditation and prayer. An unshakable foundation for life. How shall we meditate? Meditation has no boundaries. An individual adventure. First result is emotional balance. What about prayer? Daily petitions for understanding of God's will and grace to carry it out. Actual results of prayer are beyond question. Rewards of meditation and prayer.

Step Twelve

"Having had a spiritual awakening as the result of these steps, we tried to carry this message to alcoholics, and to practice these principles in all our affairs."

Joy of living is the theme of the Twelfth Step. Action its keyword. Giving that asks no reward. Love that has no price tag. What is spiritual awakening? A new state of consciousness and being is received as a free gift. Readiness to receive gift lies in practice of Twelve Steps. The magnificent reality. Rewards of helping other alcoholics. Kinds of Twelfth Step work. Problems of Twelfth Step work. What about the practice of these principles in *all* our affairs? Monotony, pain, and calamity turned to good use by practice of Steps. Difficulties of practice. "Two-stepping." Switch to "twelve-stepping" and demonstrations of faith. Growing spiritually is the answer to our problems. Placing spiritual growth first. Domination and overdependence. Putting our lives on give-and-take basis. Dependence upon God necessary to recovery of alcoholics. "Practicing these principles in *all* our affairs": Domestic relations in A.A. Outlook upon material matters changes. So do feelings about personal importance. Instincts restored to true purpose. Understanding is key to right attitudes, right action key to good living.(16)

Sexual Assault

There are about four million female alcoholics. Half may have been sexually abused in childhood. (USA Today, 1/5/98) Almost half of the female inmates in local jails—48%—have been sexually abused; more than 25% have been raped. (Associated Press 4/27/98) Sexual assault victims are more likely to attempt suicide than non-victims, especially if the assault occurred before age 16. (American Medical Association) Sexually abused children will be 27 times more likely to be arrested for prostitution as an adult than other children. (National Center for

Victims of Crime) Teenage girls who have been sexually abused are more likely to get pregnant, have poor grades and use drugs. (Associated Press, 10/1/97) As many as half of the victims of rape never fully recover and suffer lifelong chronic depression (After Silence: Rape and My Journey Back, 1998)

Sexual Assault: It's Black & White

Any forced non-consenting sexual act. This includes rape, sodomy, child sexual abuse, incest or unwanted touching. Sexual assault is about power and control. It is not about sex and certainly not about feelings of affection or love. Sexual assault is not always easy to understand and may not seem to be a black and white issue.

Misconceptions about sexual assault:

- She's just asking for trouble by dressing like that!" Nobody asks to be sexually assaulted regardless of shat he/she is wearing.

- "I bet she's lying just to get back at him!" This is a common misconception. In fact, very few reports of sexual assault are false.

- "She said 'no', but I know she really meant 'yes'." "No" means NO! Every person has the right to decide when, where and with whom she/he has sexual relations. If someone doesn't respect those decisions, it's sexual assault.

- "I've got nothing to worry about. I'm a guy!" Men and boys are not immune to sexual assault. Sexual contact without consent is sexual assault whether you're male or female.

It is estimated that one in three women and one in seven men will become the victim of some form of sexual assault in their lifetime. (14)

Incest/Sexual Abuse

If your child tells you that something happened—listen, and believe it! It is estimated that one in every three female children and one out of every seven male children will be sexually abused before reaching 18 years of age.

Child sexual abuse is no longer a secret or something that can only happen to other people. It crosses all socio-economic levels. Sex offenders come in all shapes and sizes, and from any part of society. The chance is great that the victim knows the offender.

Sexual abuse of a child is inappropriately exposing or subjecting the child to sexual contact, activity, or behavior.

This may include:

- Fondling of genitals or breasts

- Oral, vaginal or anal intercourse (penetration can be by genitals, fingers or by an object)

- Exposing sexual parts of the body

- Exposure to pornographic materials

The abuse may use physical abuse, bribery, threats, tricks, or take advantage of a younger child's lack of knowledge. When these acts occur within a family, the sexual abuse is called incest.

Child abuse prevention starts when we understand that most child molesters appear normal. (4)

Domestic Violence

Here's the weird thing about life in America. The home...which is supposed to be your sanctuary, your Number One Safe Place In The Universe...is the most dangerous place for women. Why? A lot of guys think it's OK to beat up their girlfriends and wives.

Some of these dudes put out eyes. They break bones. They turn cigarettes into branding irons. They run over their girlfriends with trucks. They rape their wives in front of the kids. They spike their beat-up lover's hospital IV with cyanide. They beat their girlfriends unconscious, put them in the trunk and drive around for days until they're brain dead. They hop out of the car and watch as the wife goes over the edge of a cliff...These are all stories that have been in the news.

And it's not just guys down on their luck. Almost every week another big name ends up on the list. Big time athletes. Hollywood stars. Doctors. Lawyers. Engineers. Politicians. Business Leaders. Neighbors who coach the kid's soccer team. Guys with more money than God...

These behind-the-scenes thugs beat up anywhere from 1 to 4 million women a year. They murder almost four women a day...more than 1,300 a year. Bottom line? Almost a third of all adult women are assaulted at least once by a partner. And it's a growing problem for teenage girls who are dating, too.

Sure, women batter. And it's a growing problem in the gay and lesbian communities. But there are A LOT MORE women who are seriously injured and killed by the men in their lives than the other way around.(7)

Attitude

"The longer I live, the more I realize the impact of attitude on life. Attitude, to me, is more important than facts. It is more important than the past, than education, than money, than circumstances, than failures, than successes, than what other people think or say or do. It is more important than appearance, giftedness or skill. It will make or break a company...a church...a home. The remarkable thing is we have a choice every day regarding the attitude we will embrace for that day. We cannot change our past...we cannot change the fact that people will act in a certain way. We cannot change the inevitable. The only thing we can do is play on the one string we have, and that is our attitude...I am convinced that life is 10% what happens to me and 90% how I react to it. And so it is with you...we are in charge of our Attitude." (2)

Incarceration

The U.S. prison population is increasing and there are more than 50,000 female inmates. More than 1/3 are in prison for a drug related offense. Forty per cent report they committed their offense while under the influence (18).

OUR SOURCES

(Bibliography)

1. *Addiction.* Treatment Handout. Author Unknown

2. *Attitude.* Treatment Handout—Author Unknown

3. Blumenthal, S. *Women and Substance Abuse: A New National Focus* in Wethington, NC and Roman, A (Eds) Drug Addiction: Research and The Health of Women. (2000) Internet 2004

4. *Child Sexual Abuse.* Pamphlet. Rape Crisis Service Planned Parenthood of the Rochester and Syracuse Region. 2004

5. *Dear Mother.* Beautiful Writings of Praise, Love and Gratitude. Hallmark p.13

6. Diamond, Jonathan, *Narrative Means to Sober Ends Treating Addiction and its Aftermath*, The Guilford Press, New York 2002 p. 227, 337.

7. *Domestic Violence.* Pamphlet. Take Back The Night March—Violence Against Women SUNY Brockport, Brockport, New York 2003.

8. *DSM IV—Diagnostic and Statistical Manual of Mental Disorders*, American Psychiatric Association 4th Edition Washington, D.C. 1994

9. *Each Day a New Beginning.* Daily Meditations for Women. Center City MN Hazelden Foundation 1991

10. *Fetal Alcohol Syndrome.* Treatment Handout Author Unknown

11. Gorski, Terrence & Miller, Marlene. *Counseling for Relapse Prevention* Independence, MO Herald House 1982 pg. 22, 44

12. *Monograph on Partners Influence on Women's Addiction and Recovery; The Connections Between Substance Abuse, Trauma, and Intimate Relationships*

National Abandoned Infants Assistance Resource Center School of Social Welfare, University of California @ Berkeley Internet 2002

13. *OASAS Twelve Core Functions* from the Office of Alcohol and Substance Abuse Services of the State of New York

14. *Rape and Sexual Assault.* Pamphlet. Planned Parenthood of the Rochester Syracuse Region 2004

15. Sutherland, Judith. *Substance Abuse Helping Women and Their Children* Internet 2002

16. *The Twelve Steps and Twelve Traditions.* Alcoholics Anonymous World Services, Inc. New York 1986

17. Townsend Claudia and Marriott, Anna Eldis. *Gender and HIV AIDS. Prevelance Among Women.* Programme at Institute of Developmental Studies University of Sussex Brighton BM 9 RE UK 2004

18. *Treatment Approaches for Women who Abuse Alcohol and Other Drugs,* Home Study Course NAR Associates, Barryville, New York 2003

19. Wegsheider—Cruz, Sharon. *Another Chance, Hope and Health for the Alcoholic Family.* Science & Behavior Books, Inc. 1981 p30,76

20. *Women and Addiction.* Gender Issues in Abuse & Treatment. Gordon, Susan Merle Caron Foundation Internet 2003

978-0-595-35817-5
0-595-35817-9